George Antheil Gives a Concert

and the audience...

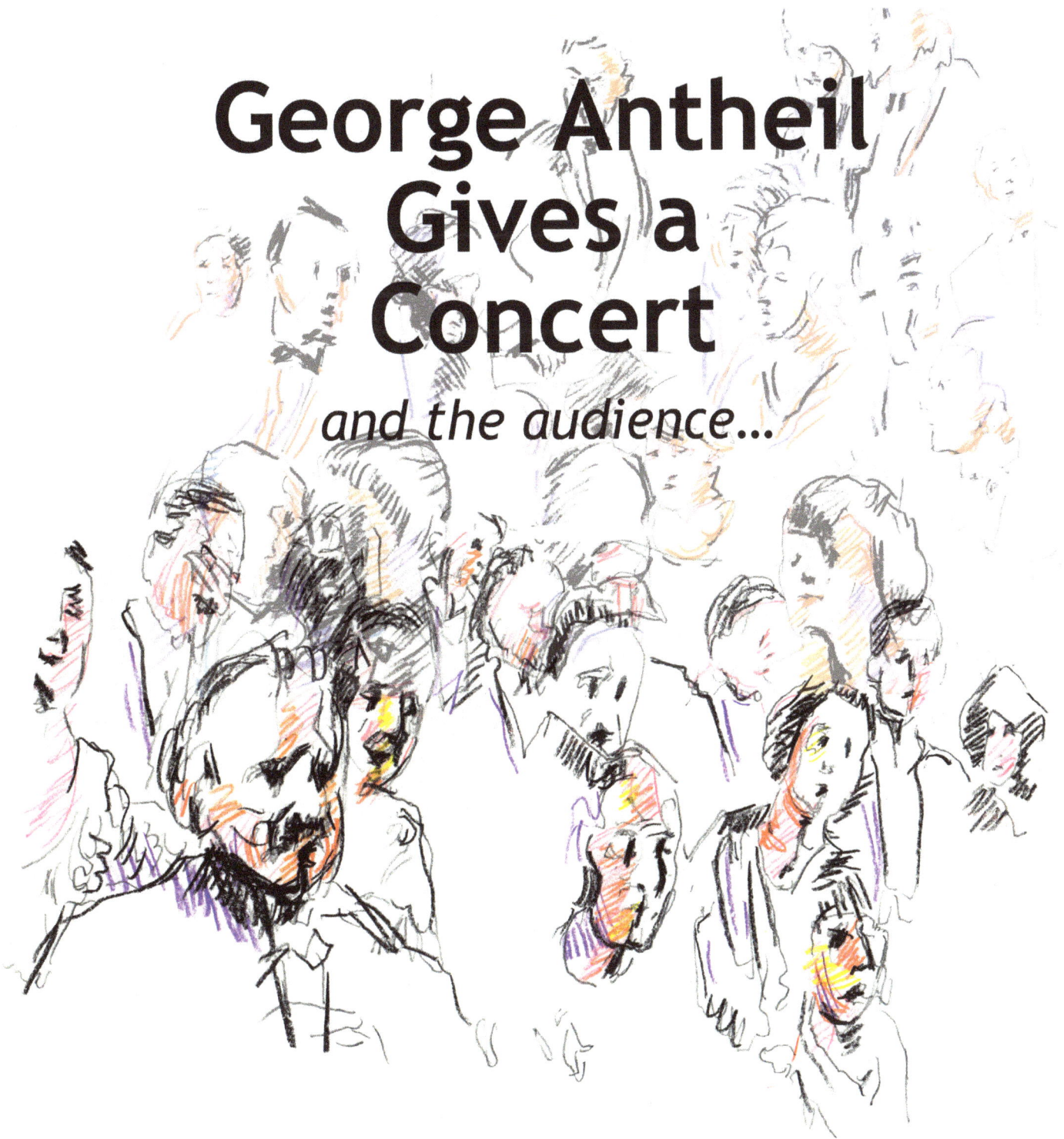

begins shouting

goes berserk

becomes unhinged !

George Antheil Gives a Concert

robert lockwood

George Antheil Gives A Concert
Copyright 2015 by Robert Lockwood

This is a work of nonfiction, and every effort has been made toward
factual accuracy. The author asks your forgiveness for any perceived
errors in this work and its portrayal of actual historical figures.

Published by Piscataqua Press
An imprint of RiverRun Bookstore
142 Fleet St., Portsmouth NH 03801

www.piscataquapress.com
www.robert-lockwood.com

ISBN: 978-1-939739-55-1

Printed in the United States of America

george antheil

pianist, composer, writer, inventor

The Bad Boy of Music

Paris
Ballet Mécanique
"The Ballet of Machines"

george antheil

The story of George Antheil and his concert

PARIS in the 1920s was a place and time when writers, musicians and artists began experimenting with new ways of expressing themselves. Imagine the freedom they felt as they found original ways to paint, sculpt, write, and compose music. It was an exciting time to be an artist and to be living in Paris — the center for artistic innovation.

George Antheil

was a child prodigy and a brilliant pianist, born in New Jersey, who became bored with classical composers such as Strauss and Debussy. He was fascinated with the experimental music of composers like Igor Stravinsky who created the radical ballets, *The Firebird* and *Rites of Spring*. George wanted to develop his own radical style. He learned that a concert manager, M.H. Hanson, was looking for a new pianist for a European concert tour so he decided to audition. To prepare he practiced 16 to 20 hours a day. When his hands swelled he soaked them in fishbowls of cold water. He won the competition and in 1920 moved to Europe to give concerts. He played everywhere. He played brilliantly. He played traditional classical pieces, as well as his own avant-garde (experimental) compositions. George's wildly aggressive piano works caused strong reactions whenever he played; in fact, they caused audiences to riot. He created chaos and pandemonium wherever he performed. He was having the time of his life.

In 1923 George settled in Paris to concentrate on composing. There he met Sylvia Beach who owned the bookstore Shakespeare and Company. The bookstore was a meeting place for many gifted and brilliant writers, artists, composers and sculptors who gathered there to discuss the latest ideas in art, literature and music.

George and his wife Boski rented a room above the bookstore. It was where he worked on his compositions. To get to his room he was sometimes seen climbing up the front wall of the bookstore to the delight of Sylvia Beach.

George charmed Sylvia Beach and she introduced him to the luminous crowd who met at her bookstore. Among those who regularly met there were the writers, James Joyce, Ernest Hemingway and Ezra Pound; the painters, Picasso, Marcel Duchamp, and Fernand Léger; the sculptors, Constantin Brancusi and Ossip Zadkine; the composer Erik Satie; the impresario Sergei Diaghilev; the photographer and filmmaker Man Ray, and Jean Cocteau, poet, novelist, dramatist, designer, playwright, artist and filmmaker.

A less likely ensemble of people (poets, painters, prophets) could hardly be imagined.

james joyce

fernand léger

The Builder by Léger

ossip zadkine

ernest hemingway

"If you are lucky enough to have lived in Paris, as a young man, then wherever you go for the rest of your life it stays with you, for Paris is a moveable feast."

Ernest Hemingway

igor stravinsky

ezra pound

Stravinsky by Picasso

f. scott
fitzgerald

constantin
brancusi

"Almost any noun
is better alone than chaperoned
if it's the right noun, and very few
can stand two adjectives.
'Unsettled dream' is
stronger than
'unsettled white dream.'"

Ezra Pound

pablo
picasso

The Kiss by Brancusi

The Ballet Mécanique

For George, it was a creative and productive time and
he soon completed his most ambitious and radical piece,
the Ballet mécanique. Sylvia Beach didn't much like the name.
She pointed out to George that if you changed the French
spelling of the first word a little, Ballet mécanique becomes
Balai mécanique — meaning mechanical broom or carpet
sweeper. "I'll write a piece about a carpet sweeper," he
replied, enjoying the play on words.

George described his compositions as "ultramodern." They were
aggressive, dissonant, percussive — very different from what
people were used to hearing. The Ballet mécanique, his Magnum
Opus (Great Work), called for 16 synchronized player pianos and
a percussion orchestra made up of three xylophones, four bass
drums, a tam-tam (a gong with indefinite pitch), seven
electric bells, a siren, and three airplane propellers.

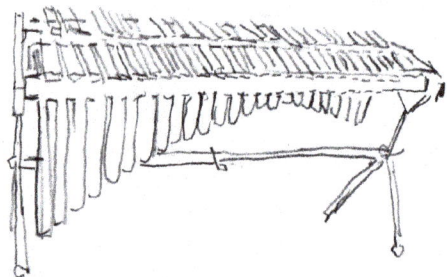

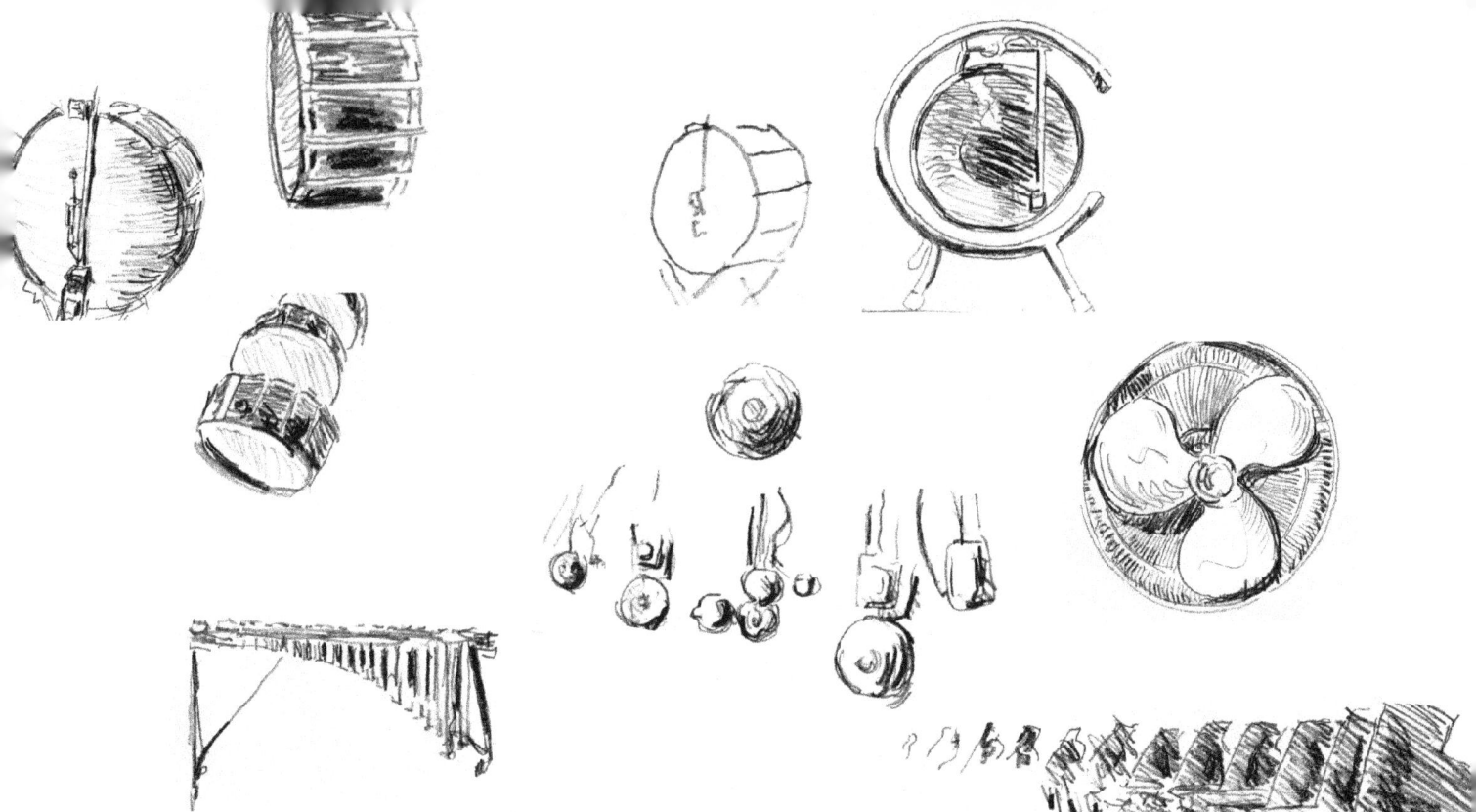

There was a problem, however. The technology for synchronizing 16 player pianos and getting them all to play together didn't exist. So George settled for just one player piano, and eight grand pianos with human performers. From hardware stores came saws, hammers, electric bells and fans to replace the airplane propellers.

The Theatre

To generate publicity for the concert George gave semi-private previews. A headline in one Paris newspaper read "Ballet mécanique to wipe out big orchestras, and audiences, too." For the grand premiere George hired the French conductor of the Ballet Russe, Vladimir Golschmann. He arranged for the event to be held at the grand **Theatre des Champs-Elysees,** a beautiful 2,500-seat art nouveau concert hall.

Theatre des Champs-Elysees designed by *architects Henry Van de Velde and Auguste Perret, painter and sculptor Antoine Bourdelle, painter Maurice Denis, and designer René Lalique.*

Art Nouveau means "new art." It features naturalistic
but stylized forms, geometric shapes, arcs, and
semi-circles. The works incorporate
natural forms like flowers, weeds,
and even fairies.

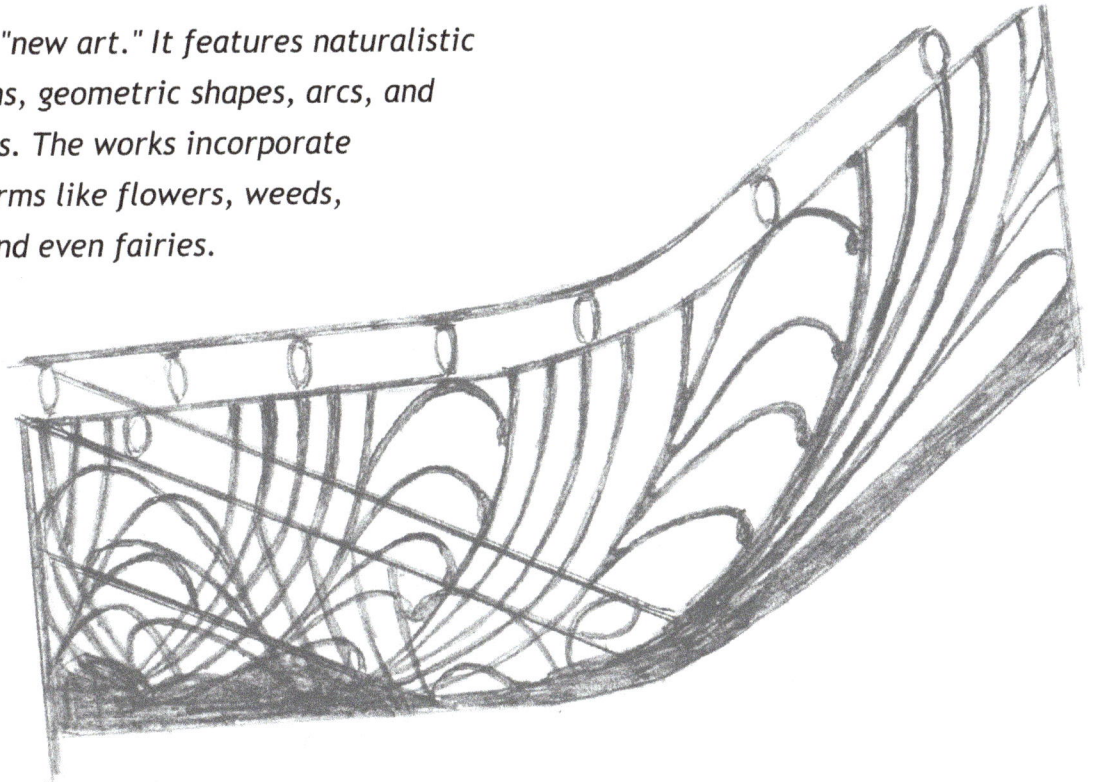

The Concert

At the concert on June 19, 1926, George's friends and supporters came out in force. Among those in attendance at the theatre were Ezra Pound, James Joyce and T.S.Eliot. Also, Princess di Bassiano, publisher of the literary journal "Botteghe Oscure;" the playwright, poet and novelist Natalie Barney; Sylvia Beach with her friend the poet Adrienne Monnier; the Boston Symphony Orchestra conductor Serge Koussevitzky; the writer William Shirer; the poet Pierre Minet; the playwright, poet and novelist Djuna Barnes; Emmanuel Rudnitsky, alias Man Ray, and Alice Prin, alias Kiki of Montparnasse, model, actress and painter, and Antheil's protegee Bravig Imbs.

The theatre was packed.

sylvia beach

adrienne monnier

t.s. eliot

pierre minet

djuna barnes

natalie barney

man ray

kiki de montparnasse

sergei diaghilev

Say goodbye to harmony

Because most of George's concerts caused a riot, it's no surprise that this event would begin in a most unfortunate way. George's friend Bravig Imbs best captures the zany wildness of the event with this wry account:

"There was a great deal of fuss while the orchestra arranged itself for this event. George appeared on the stage, pale and nervous, giving crisp directions to the movers who were pushing five pianos into place, and to the electricians who were arranging a loudspeaker to amplify the small electric fans that took the place of the airplane propellers. All these operations variously **provoked fear, pity and amusement in the audience.** Finally, George nodded his head as a cue to Golschmann that everything was ready and sat down at his piano with a grim expression on his face.

"Within a few minutes, the concert became sheer bedlam. Above the mighty noise of the pianos and drums arose cat-calls and booing, shrieking and whistling, shouts of 'thief' mixed with 'bravo.' People began to call each other names and to forget that there was any music going on at all. I suffered with George, wishing that people would have at least the courtesy to stay quiet, but Golschmann was so furious he would not give up his baton, and continued to conduct imperturbably as though he were the dead center of a whirlpool.

"I caught the general fever of unrest myself. 'Do keep quiet, please,' I said to some of my particularly noisy neighbors. 'Shut your face, yourself,' they answered, and then started whistling which is the supreme form of contempt in France.

"Then, for an instant, there was a curious lull in the clamor and Ezra Pound took advantage of it to jump to his feet and yelled, '*Vous etes tous des imbeciles!*'

"He was shouted down from the gallery, of course, with many vulgar epithets, and the music continued monotonously and determinedly.

"The *Ballet* began to seem to me like some monstrous abstract beast, battling with the nerves of the audience, and I began to wonder which would win out....

Vous êtes tous des imbéciles'

"The opposition reached its climax, though, when the loud-speaker began to function. It made as much noise as a dozen airplanes, and no amount of shouting could drown it completely. One fat bald old gentleman who had been particularly disagreeable would not be balked by this, however, and to the glee of the audience, lashed out his umbrella, opened it and pretended to be struggling against the imaginary gale of wind from the electric fans. His gesture was immediately copied by many more people in the audience until the theatre seemed decked with quite a sprinkling of black mushrooms.

"Of course, when the Ballet was over, George got an ovation which was greater than the cat-calls, for everyone was willing to applaud a man who had at least accomplished something. He bowed and blushed and blushed and bowed and all his friends were very proud of him."

Think about what it must have been like on that hot June night in Paris with that glittering, riotous, crazy crowd, packed together in the beautiful art nouveau concert hall, Theatre des Champs-Elysees, for the first time experiencing the disturbing charm of the new — "The Ballet of Machines."

Postscript

A year after the Paris concert George and Boski were in New York for a Carnegie Hall performance of the "Ballet mécanique." But the reception in New York was even more disastrous than in Paris. The critics ridiculed the ballet, and the audience was outraged and intimidated by it. A real airplane propeller was found as a prop for the concert. Larger fans were used for the propeller noises, and they were pointed at the audience, not up in the air as they had been in Paris. No one opened their umbrella as protection from the ferocious wind as was done in Paris, but someone did hold up his cane with a hankerchief tied to it as a sign of surrender.

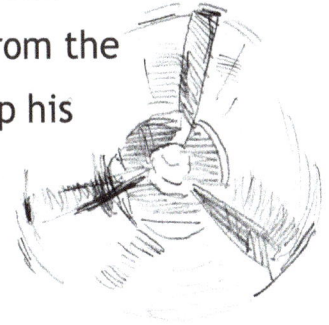

George and Boski returned to Paris where he changed his approach to composing in a more lyrical style. He wrote operas and more conventional pieces. Three years after settling in Paris he and his wife moved back to the United States. He eventually made his home in Hollywood where, with the movie star Hedy Lamarr, he invented a technology that led to wireless phones, GPS systems and numerous other modern inventions. He wrote music for more than thirty films. There were no more riots.

The
end

To find out more about George Antheil

pronounced "ANN-tile"

In Hollywood George Antheil wrote music for popular film directors like Cecil B. DeMille. He said most background scores for films were "unmitigated tripe". He was more interested in independent producers such as Ben Hecht. He wrote the scores for *Angels Over Broadway* (1940) and *Specter of the Rose* (1946). He also wrote the score for the independent film *Dementia* which contains no dialogue, only music, and is thought by critics to be his finest work.

www.antheil.org (Paul Lehrman's comprehensive website on the Ballet Mécanique.)
DVD, "Bad Boy Made Good," Electronic Music Foundation, Albany, NY, 2006
(badboymadegood.com)

www.paristransatlantic.com/antheil/mainpage/resource html

Hedy's Folly, Richard Rhodes, Vintage Books, New York, 2011.

Antheil and the Treatise on Harmony, Ezra Pound, 1923.

Bad Boy of Music, George Antheil. Garden City, New York: Doubleday, 1945.

Four Lives in Paris, Hugh Ford. North Point Press, San Francisco, 1987.

Sylvia Beach and the Lost Generation, Noel Riley Fitch. W. W. Norton, 1983.

Shakespeare & Company, New York, Sylvia Beach, Harcourt Brace, 1959.

Confessions of Another Young Man, Bravig Imbs, New York, Henkle-Yewdale, 1936.

The Mechanical Angel: His Adventures and Enterprises in the Glittering 1920s, Donald Friede,

New York, Alfred A. Knopf, 1948.

Art and Modernism in the United States, Townsend Ludington, Editor. See page 175, George Antheil's Ballet Mecanique and Transatlantic Modernism, Carol J. Oja, The University of North Carolina Press, Chapel Hill & London, 2000.

Learn more about...

james joyce

James Joyce was an Irish modernist writer who wrote in a stream of consciousness style. Because of the explicit content of his work it was banned in England and the United States. Sylvia Beach published his ground-breaking work "Ulysses."
www.biography.com/people/james-joyce-9358676

fernand léger

Fernand Léger created abstract paintings that combined elements of Cubism with his own style of using forms as tubular cylinders. In 1924, Léger with Man Ray made the film, Ballet Mécanique.
www.biography.com/people/fernand-l%C3%A9ger-39474

ossip zadkine

Ossip Joselyn Zadkine studied art in London and settled in Paris around 1910. He applied the principles of Cubism with a style that was influenced by African art.
www.zadkine.com/writing/new-york-times

ernest hemingway

Nobel Prize winner Ernest Hemingway is considered one of the great American 20th century novelists, and is known for works like A Farewell to Arms, The Sun Also Rises and The Old Man and the Sea.
www.biography.com/people/ernest-hemingway-9334498

igor stravinsky

Stravinsky achieved international fame with the ballet, The Firebird (1910), commissioned by the impresario Sergei Diaghilev and performed in Paris by Diaghilev's Ballets Russes.

en.wikipedia.org/wiki/Igor-Stravinsky

f. scott fitzgerald

Fitzgerald wrote short stories, novels, and later in life turned to screenwriting. He led a personal life of excess and is known for his most famous novel, The Great Gatsby.

www.biography.com/people/f-scott-fitzgerald-9296261

ezra pound

Poet Ezra Pound wrote more than 70 books and influenced many other writers, including James Joyce and T.S. Eliot. His poetry was influenced by visual art forms such as Cubism.

www.biography.com/people/ezra-pound-9445428

constantin brancusi

Constantin Brancusi's sculpture is noted for its visual elegance and sensitive use of materials, with the directness of peasant carving and the sophistication of the Parisian avant-garde.

www.brancusi.com/bio.html

pablo picasso

Pablo Picasso with Georges Braque created Cubism, a style that influenced the direction of modern art. His painting, "Les Demoiselles d'Avignon," is credited with taking art into a new and radical direction from the past.

www.biography.com/people/pablo-picasso-9440021

sylvia beach

Artists and writers tired of censorship and rejection in their own country fled to Paris's left bank artistic and literary scene. Writers James Joyce, Ernest Hemingway, and Ezra Pound met at Sylvia Beach's Shakespeare and Company.

www.thehemingwayproject.com/in-praise-of-sylvia-beach/

adrienne monnier

French poet, bookseller and publisher Adrienne Monnier, Sylvia's friend, also provided a meeting place for artists and writers at her bookstore La Maison des Ais des Livres.

http://leblog1815.blogspot.com/2011/03/sylvia-beach.html

t.s. eliot

Eliot's poem "The Love Song of J.Alfred Prufrock" established him as a leading poet of his day. He founded and edited the exclusive and influential literary journal Criterion.

www.nobelprize.org/nobel_prizes/literature/laureates/1948/eliot-bio.html

djuna barnes

Poet, novelist, playwright and illustrator Barnes wrote articles for such magazines as Vanity Fair, and The New Yorker. She was a part of the modernist scene in Paris. Her poems and novels influenced many other writers of her era.

http://www.studiocleo.com/librarie/barnes/djunabarnes.html

pierre minet

Minet was a French writer and poet known for his book *Circoncision du Coeur (circumcision of the heart)*.

books.google.com/books?isbn=1590171845

kiki de montparnasse

Alice Ernestine Prin, nicknamed Queen of Montparnasse, and often known as Kiki de Montparnasse, was a French artist's model, nightclub singer, actress, memoirist and painter.
www.google.com/search?q=alice+prin

natalie barney

Natalie Clifford Barney was an American playwright, poet and novelist who lived as an extravagant expatriate in Paris.
www.jstor.org/stable/3173396

sergei diaghilev

Sergei Diaghilev was a Russian artistic visionary and founder of Ballets Russes, which profoundly shaped the course of the dance/performance world.
www.biography.com/people/sergei-diaghilev-37296

man ray

Emmanuel Rudnitsky. Photographer, painter and filmmaker, Man Ray lived in Paris in the 1920's and 1930's, where he played a key role in the Dada and Surrealist movements.
www.manraytrust.com/

bravig imbs

Bravig Imbs was a novelist, poet and a memoirist and was friends with George Antheil, Gertrude Stein and Alice B. Toklas.
www.poemhunter.com/bravig-imbs/

To Nancy

my wife, best friend
and editor.

www.ingramcontent.com/pod-product-compliance
Lightning Source LLC
Chambersburg PA
CBHW040853100426
42813CB00015B/2788